Seedling

*(a garden of poems exploring self discovery,
childhood trauma, love, and everything in between.)*

Sarah Joannidi

Seedling
Copyright © 2021 Sarah Joannidi

Produced and printed by Stillwater River Publications. All rights reserved. Written and produced in the United States of America. This book may not be reproduced or sold in any form without the expressed, written permission of the author(s) and publisher.

Visit our website at
www.StillwaterPress.com
for more information.

First Stillwater River Publications Edition

ISBN: 978-1-955123-58-7

12345678910
Written by Sarah Joannidi
Cover Art by Matthew St. Jean
Published by Stillwater River Publications,
Pawtucket, RI, USA.

The views and opinions expressed in this book are solely those of the author(s) and do not necessarily reflect the views and opinions of the publisher.

Dedication

For those who will read this
and for my husband Nick,
who has always been my saving grace.

Seedling

Contents

Neighbors	1	Father Sun	28
Seedling	2	Lay Still	30
Describe You	3	I See You	31
Other Skin	4	Restless One	32
Quiet Dark	5	I Am Present	33
Darkest Spaces	6	Pieces of a Heart	34
In Them All	7	Amidst the Noise	35
Hope	8	Brave and Small	36
Into the Water	9	Strong Woman	38
My Castle	10	Welcome	39
Seven Ships	11	Strange	40
If You Can't	12	Virus	41
My Words	13	Going In Blind	42
Her Heart	14	A Little at a Time	43
Long Winter	15	Envy and Awe	44
Let It Be	16	When She Goes	45
If It Ever Were	17	False Hope	46
Hunted	18	Call Me Chaos	47
Twenty Years From Now	19	Wouldn't It Be Lovely	48
Castle	20	Constant Reminders	49
Girls Like Us	21	Dragons of a Heart	50
Impure	22	After All This Time	51
Part of Me	23	It's Hard to Believe	52
Beyond Me	24	Beside the Glass	53
Come What May	25	You Cannot Write	
Rather Lovely	26	My Story	54
Mother Moon	27	Like Gin	55

Though You May Not Remember	56	Vulnerable	68
Home Town	57	A Letter to My Life	69
If Nothing Else	58	Elementary	70
Only the Taken	59	She Has Bloomed	71
Pills and Promises	60	Who Am I in Your Story?	72
Like a Beast	61	Life	73
Never In My Life	62	This River Runs	74
Origin Story	63	Close the Window	75
Shatter Me	65	Chipping Blue	76
After All	66	Who Saves You	77
To Remember You By	67		

Neighbors

we engage in the awkward dance of
gardening and waving
while elusive eye contact escapes us
and the sea of mailboxes
acts as a barrier between us
we watch the lights flicker
at respective hours
behind windows holding curtains
neither of us will ever see
we are strangers
we are neighbors
but it makes no difference to me

Seedling

how many seeds I've planted
hoping to watch you bloom
how many nights I've prayed
to the forest, to the moon
I won't waiver, waiting
trusting you will find me soon

Describe You

describe you they said
like words could create
an image of you
outside of my own head
I opened clean pages
uncapped a new pen
and the smell of coffee
and garlic
and jazz in the kitchen
consumed each line
you are so guarded
to the world around you
and so open
and lovely
with me
I am a woman of words
until they ask me
to pour you onto a page
and suddenly I am reduced
to the sweet silence
that is loving you
choosing to save our travels and trails
and the jokes that you tell
for my own selfish consumption

Other Skin

sometimes I try on other skin
feel the cracks and folds
let myself in

I feel the textures
smell the smoke
admire pictures on the wall
feel the love swell
in my unfamiliar heart
as I spend a moment with them all

the memories in these hands
are not mine to be remembered
I am only an observer here
to this ink I have been tethered

I wear the skin
try on the bones
find myself another home

to wear on paper
to feel in my soul
through the experience of others
I am me
and you
and whole

Quiet Dark

when it's quiet,
dark
and empty
life is brimming just beneath—
it's hard to feel it in those moments
but those moments aren't for peace
and so we find
our hearts are lonely
and our eyes are filled with fear
but when the season passes, darling,
only love will find us here.

Darkest Spaces

the darkest spaces
filled with light
dripping in sin
can't make it right

your face is deception
but for you, that's the fun,
and here lie the rest of us
coming undone

In Them All

I see me in you,
she said
to the empty mirror standing tall
I see me in you
she said
I see me in them all

Hope

there's a sea that pours her heart out
into the shallows of the sand
all her pain is buried there
where the water meets the land.

in the middle of the ocean
there's a ship that's lost at sea
buried in the waves beneath
the man he used to be.

and somewhere just between them
is a bottle filled with hope
that will likely never find them as it fights to stay afloat.

Into the Water

into the water fast; blind, breathless, drowning,
out the sounds of pain, wishing love had never found me
waves crash over my head, the bottoms too deep to touch
on my back I float off further, this has become too much

this was not my plan for me, I told you from the start
I didn't want to love you, I was supposed to save my heart.
but you have it and you hold it,
currently crushing it with your ice,
so I choose the water now, I cannot live a lover's life.
I will let the waves crash over me until I find my calm,
and our love will find its way to us when the storm is done.
this love is greater than us, running its own course,
and we are just the vessels for an old and powerful force.

the storm will pass, as it always does and all will soon be well,
but I need to float for now, I need peace within myself.
we cannot force, cannot pry, cannot grasp before it's time,
this is true, this is my lesson; this love is our life.

My Castle

my castle built of feathers and dreams,
is slowly crashing down on me.
my stained glass windows have turned black,
with fear and apprehension,
the view beyond them has escaped
and left me here to question.
if all my doubts were worth their while,
as I see they have collected,
and taken more than they promised to give,
leaving my castle unprotected.
so I stand atop my tower looking for any hope at all,
but all around me and beneath me gathers fast to fall.
and I am sinking slowly as my castle turns to smoke,
dressed in dreams that could've been,
beneath a nightmare's cloak.
left with the rubble and the dust of all my fearless dreams,
feathers falling, demons crawling,
new walls form from screams.
stained glass windows are now bars, my tower is a tomb,
and here I'll stay until I learn to never let doubt into the room.

Seven Ships

when seven other ships have sailed,
when all the other lives have passed,
you'll search again, you'll want me then,
when all that's green is not your grass.
when the sun has set and the moon has risen
for your one hundredth night alone,
you'll find a window and beg a star to light your way;
to lead you home.
when the shadows cast on your wall,
have become to you familiar,
you'll remember me but have only them;
an empty rooms ghostly figures.
when the road you've traveled turns out
to be nothing but mud and rivers,
when the home you've lost has left your dreams
and marks you a taker of givers.
then you will know, almost a little
of the pain you've never known,
and you will feel, with almost compassion,
for the hearts you took with the coldness of stone.
oh, but until then may your seas be calm,
may your grass be green and your days be long
may your fickle heart be vain and free,
and may you never love a wretch like me.
know that beauty will fade,
and lies unravel like red hands on a heart,
because this truth will reveal you
and leave you with only the ugly you are.

If You Can't

and if you can't beat em' join em'
they say with such straight faces,
sharing our homes with strangers; our beds like public places.
lonely are we in the crowds,
buzz on, "checked in," and tuned out.
status updates, Instagram—this has become our
lives, selfies, Twitter, YOLO; forever online.
consensual silence—the damnation of humanity,
we are close but strangers—why haven't we learned anything?
we're letting go, we're losing touch,
to stay in touch we're giving up.
saddened are our forefathers if they're anywhere to see,
for all they lived and fought for; our current tragedy.
heartless love, and I is A,
always first but last to stay.
lives so interchangeable, everything replaceable,
nothing's unexplainable,
except what we've come to be,
a world at our fingertips, potion for love in several sips, words
that never touch our lips—
this is humanity.
and if you can't beat em' join em' is the stance we seem to take,
but while doing so we fail to see—
this will be our greatest mistake.

My Words

my words are falling, splashing like rain on hot black tar,
forming puddles of description that are deeper than they are.
scattered and unorganized, lovely and unspoken,
spring rain calm and winter rain frozen.
they find families between themselves, spaces in each stanza,
where they belong innately and I am just a cancer.
spreading words like disease on the prettiest of pages,
splattered ink, stark and black—but not contagious.
falling from my pen, like rain, like love, like cancer,
are all my words, my questions, crashing—
like graceful dancers.
 putrid as death, sweet as a lover
they find their places within each other.
and my ivory page is dressed in black—
behold the colors it screams,
showing me like a hologram all of my wildest dreams
the ink like paint that will never dry
the page; a canvas—vast as the sky.
my words, my children, my own disease,
have settled here; they've been released.

Her Heart

her beating heart pounds like a drum to no tune,
lost in the haze of a summer afternoon.
her pulse vibrates through her wrists—begging for attention,
as her mind dances madly around fear and apprehension.
her dark eyes glow with the light of the moon,
as the heat of the sun leaves behind a cold room.
her bare feet kiss the hardwood floors,
as she stands facing the slamming doors.
the walls are shifting and shaping—she's lost within these halls,
the sun is gone, shadows instigate, she can hear nothing at all.
her heart starts to scream pounding through her chest
as if searching too—
for a way to be calm, a way to be free,
a way to escape this room.
the curtains like men of wicked nature,
reach out to touch her, to grab her, to taint her.
by the force of foreign power she is frozen in her bones,
as the doors, the walls, the curtains
vow to take her as their own.
the splinters slither beneath her feet and prick their way
through her skin,
pain washes over her as the floorboards crack and pull her in.
the walls shift rapid, the curtains chant
and mock her all the while,
the doors slam angry, violent above her—
beneath her skin the splinters smile.

Long Winter

it was a long cold winter, with snow into April
and frost into May,
June found us anxious for summer's long days.
pale faced natives in sweaters and shorts,
claiming this was the longest winter for sure.
soon the days will be warmer and the flowers will bloom,
and we'll be saying all summer "winter's coming soon."
we'll bask in the warmth and take pride in our gardens,
before winter's icy breath forces them to harden.
they are fleeting, the other three—the seasons we so love
we could spend forever with them but it'd never be enough.
we long for Spring; mother of birth, Summer;
daughter of flowers,
for Autumn a favorite of most, a time for color filled showers
like the faithful lovers of soldiers at war, we are to our seasons,
and we stay here waiting, every year,
for that old New England reason.

Let It Be

let it be—
they say to me
like it's simple
like I'm strong.
but you've been lost
and I've been searching
for far too long.
and here we are
new fight
new day
and I have to let go in a whole new way.

I had you for a moment
a tiny space in time
but I cling to when the father that I had was mine.

let it go
they tell me
I tell myself the same,
but still I cling to hoping that
somehow you will change.

If It Ever Were

if it ever were or could be again,
it'll be the best it ever had been.
I'd find your soul be it centuries from mine,
our love immeasurable through distance and time.
my heart would know you if my eyes could not see,
I'd feel you if nothing were left of me.
through the darkest of black and the brightest of white,
I will know you and love you in all of my lives.
if love is immortality—our love proves that to be,
no life, no death, no circumstance could ever get between.
the binding of our love, our souls are intertwined,
be it this world or the next—your soul I'll always find.
every life will be a journey to get to where you are,
simply as souls or being to being,
I've found my home inside your heart.
from then to now, from here to then,
a love like ours will know no end.

Hunted

I heard the twigs snap
the leaves crack
the arrow grazed my skin
I smelled the copper and the wonder
in the wind as it rushed in
I felt you watching
perched in waiting
marveled by my plight
I'll take your arrow
and raise you a wolf
born and brazen for this fight.

Twenty Years From Now

we would sit with
strawberrylip gloss
being passed between us like
alcohol soon would be
we would speak of the future
like it were a fairy tale
not knowing yet, that evil step mothers and deep forests
were just around the corner.
when we imagined twenty years from then, we were babies
and here the years have found us, with and without our babies.
twenty years from now, we'll be a little more lined
a little more wise
but we'll never be snug in glitter and butterfly clips
holding tight to secrets
that belonged only to us, again.

Castle

when I was small
I screamed
silently for a castle

not to fill it with pretty things
or to be saved by a prince
but to have my own watch tower
where I could listen and observe
unassumingly from my perch

when I grew up I discovered
I need only to be a bird
I'd let the branches do my bidding
and greet the vastness of the sky
with my eagerness to explore

no need for that castle anymore.

Girls Like Us

everything I owned was used
girls like us aren't much like you

Impure

impure, imperfect and infectiously ridden,
with a past of unholy and impulsive decisions.
unaware, naive, a shallow hearts rhythm,
dancing in circles around its satisfied prison.
unruly, flaming, righteous fire,
struck by the match of the most burning desire.
drenched in the deathly sweet smell of lust,
drowning in oceans of misconceived trust.
distanced by love and all of its glory,
tangled in the romance of every story.
impure, detached, yet content in this living,
will the lovers be lovers devout beyond giving?

Part of Me

there's a part of me I found in you, in those familiar eyes,
there's a calm in you that resonates and stilled my stormy life.
there's a deeper love than what I've known,
between your heart and mine,
there's this knowing that I can't explain—
this boundless sense of time.
there is more to this than we both know, I feel it in my soul,
it's more than a partnership—this new love is somehow old.
we are air together—fire flaming through the ice,
we are well together—meant to be—travelers through life.
we are a story, a painting, a poem,
out of reach and reason our love is it's own.
we have sunk anchors, burned scars, claimed hearts,
and this love has cast us it's two leading parts.
here's to a good show, to the best role,
here's to every stage with you,
I'll love you in this life and the next
with a love familiar and new.

Beyond Me

beyond me and beyond words is a place just for our love,
when in its purest form being is enough.
as if your print were needed to get beyond the locks,
you're the only one who's been behind the caging of my heart.
before you there was a tunnel within a cave within a cage,
that called itself my heart and kept it dark, refusing change.
before you it was cold here with summers lost in snow,
and the cave that was my heart was for nobody to know.
then came the day you found a shadow of a feeling
that you knew,
and you explored a cave that freed and led my heart to you.
and in every moment since the choice I never made,
I've been lost in crazy love with you and somehow know
that it won't change.
love was the shadow on our hearts
that led our souls to life,
now may forever be with you love, it's with you that I'm alive.

Come What May

come what may my love you know you'll always be,
my life, my love, my partner, my immortality.
should life or death dare come between what is ours
and ours alone,
they shall know the wrath of immortal love,
like so few have ever known.
the skies would roar with angry thunder
and strike lightning down in vain,
the seas would flood with lover's blood
 who know the kind of pain.
that only lovers of the many worlds have ever come to know,
and the earth would fight for us love,
with a motive all of her own.
armies of trees would stand against the many wicked ways,
a battle would become of this, so many things would change.
fields of glory would stand strong and offer safe harbor for us,
as the earth, our mother fights for the sake of our love.
our idle bodies would lay at rest hand in hand—souls at flight,
to join our mother in the battle for our love and we would fight.
the sky would play our lives like a silent film in the clouds,
and the many ways we've loved
would be clear to see from every ground.
and there we'd stand with our mother—
our love and souls combining,
and we would win the battle of love—everlasting and undying.
oh, come what may my love you know you'll always be,
my life, my love, my partner, my immortality.

Rather Lovely

I found you rather lovely, in a broken-hearted way,
in a dress made of flower petals on the most ordinary of days.
your chestnut hair tousled and long,
dancing to your own made up song.
sharing tales forever tall, standing against the wind,
arms as open as your heart, lovely as you'd ever been.
your eyes revealed your smile before your lips could even curl,
and in your presence I was enthralled
by the world's most beautiful girl.
I saw a world in your eyes and became a lover of dreams,
I spent a day with you and realized nothing was as it seemed.
there's a part of me I found with you,
that you seemed to know was there,
you're my discover girl—
dressed in petals and windblown hair.
you stumbled into my life falling into me with grace,
and I will never be as I was before
I knew the curves of your face.

Mother Moon

how long has the moon been watching
as my tears collect in pools
how many nights has the moon bore witness
to my fondness for fools
if mother moon adores me
why does she let me cry
and wish and wonder often,
and leave me asking why?

Father Sun

to the moon and sun and back again—the same one we all see,
in a world as vastly small as this it's the same air we all breathe.
we dance to the rhythms in our hearts—
and in each heart resides,
different tunes, and different blood—
but in this way we are alike.
the soil in our hands will dry, the birds above us will always fly,
the sun and moon in one big sky
but here on land we differ?
basic needs to eat and breathe
to plant our roots—to stay or leave
a love for love that comes naturally,
but we are dying quicker.
dying in a way of life that most consider living,
cold and judging everyone tirelessly unforgiving.
more accepting in so many ways—or have we just accepted,
that there are many kinds of people that are better off rejected?
in a time where love is legal and grass is fine to smoke,
you'd think we'd have a better understanding,
but understand we don't.

we are multiplying, manipulating, and burying our souls,
amongst the wilted elders who tried to help us grow.
we plant our weeds beside the oaks and say we saved the forest,
but there's nothing that we're doing
and nothing can be done for us.
we are frozen souls in bodies running wild,
beneath the same moon and sun we've become the dying child.
now our mother moon must watch while father sun sets,
over a sea that has been flooded
with the souls he couldn't protect.

Lay Still

lay still, be calm, listen and let go,
be aware of what is greater; accept that you don't know.
don't push what you should not,
have faith that keeps you grounded,
there is much to be considered
but you will know once you've found it.
be humble, be happy, and find peace amongst the pain,
regret nothing, accept fault, and know that love is not a game.
to be happy is a challenge—it is a daily choice,
in all of your suffering do not ever lose your voice.
know you matter and that you don't—know the world is vast,
know your own soul and know it well—
it's the only part that lasts.
and when you love, love true and strong,
and when you love yourself you will always belong.
open your heart, and close your eyes;
let go
let go
let go
believe, be strong, and fully accept that it is okay not to know.

I See You

there you are I see you still,
sitting by that window sill
dreaming, wishing, eyes to the sky,
a bird in your mind; free to fly.
in that room you're behind those walls,
and I find you there every time I feel small.
because there was sadness, madness, fear
and there is none of that now—none of that here.
there were watchful eyes—there was doubt and despair,
but here, you've made it out of there.
when life is too much and even seconds seem long,
I find strength in then; where you became strong.
all of then makes any of now seem so simple, so minute,
when I need my strength, I go back to that room—
that window
and I remember you.

Restless One

Settle down dear restless one, all that should will be,
You cannot rush and you cannot force
or your decisions will not be free.
All in due time love, as you already know—
Imagine the places your heart may still go
Stones are a burden when used as an anchor
for all things meant to be flying,
No doubt your effort will count in the end
but some things aren't meant for trying.
You must allow what will, to be on its own,
because it is here mistakes may thrive,
You must be patient, love entirely—
and you must always be kind.
Trust in the plan for you, trust in your heart,
and allow your mind some slack,
Because all of those "musts" and "must nots"
will take what you'll never get back.
Relax here love—settle down, this is your life after all,
Allow your heart to guide you
and your trust will be there should you fall.
Learn to find comfort where comfort is foreign
and you'll have found success,
My advice to your heart—guide purely, love truly,
do not over protect.
Let in, let go, let be what may,
And be free in life and love
always.

I Am Present

I am present in this moment; I am aware,
I am without worry though not without care.
I am conscious of my breath; slow and deep,
I am letting go of attachments I need not keep.
I surrender to this moment; I give peace to my soul,
deserving, free flying, centuries old.
namaste, honor, serenity, and calm,
I release myself as I bring together my palms.
I yield to this moment for all after and before,
are not here yet or anymore.
I love and breathe and always will be,
alive in the present—eternally.

Pieces of a Heart

there are pieces of a heart that can never be replaced,
there are parts in every story that will always take place.
there is nothing forgotten that would have been remembered,
there is no such time as "once upon forever."
there is no escaping what fate has predetermined,
there is no preacher with a magical sermon.
there is only this and what we each believe,
that takes part in our choices and the lives that we lead.
as for what is real or not—we may never know,
we have only our minds—and all the places it will go.

Amidst the Noise

alive in all the ways one can be—silent amidst the noise,
vibrant inside the wind and rain—
through the storm always poised.
watchful of the hummingbird drinking nectar by the bees,
enchanted by the act of this—oh sweet simplicity.
comforted by the wolves sharing secrets with the moon,
serene inside the open fields on a lazy afternoon.
centered safe beneath the trees; rooted as they are,
calm as the leaves rustle softly beneath the stars.
content inside the sunshine's rays—
patiently waiting for the blue,
there is magic like no other when the sun bows
to greet the moon.
a single wish for every soul—to slow and to simply be,
enjoy the blue while it is present—
in those moments you will see.

Brave and Small

there she stood so brave and small,
being the strongest of them all.
a shattered home of guilty lies,
of lovely, sinful, sad goodbyes.
brothers, sister, mother and father,
things being taken and exchanged around her.
but there she stood within those walls,
always the bravest of them all.
the woman that she grew to be,
built on love, strength, and integrity.
she stood so fair, so kind and bold,
a young woman with a soul so old.
the beauty and persistence—the love within her heart,
she found it on her own—the drive to never fall apart.
when the castles crumbled and the bricks did fall,
there stood she—strongest of them all.
she kept her stance on shaky ground,
she held her head high when the shades were down.
the beauty that her soul contains—
the strength within her bones
have led her through this life carving her path in stones.
though times change and dreams may vary—
wind rustles fallen leaves too,
and she finds the strength every time to do what she must do.
through the storm she remains unshaken,
through the rain she's embraced the thunder,

through the pain she's found the beauty
and through her struggles she has discovered,
that life will be just as it may—
presenting obstacles big and small,
but no matter the battle she's ready to fight—
for she is the strongest of them all.

Strong Woman

in all the years I've known you,
I've never known you like this year,
stronger in your soul you seem, stronger than your fear.
the faith I'd gained and lost in you, I've gained in you again,
and these may be some dark times, but darker there have been.
you survived the fire, you conquered crumbling walls,
now stand there on your mountain
and watch your demons fall.
this is you, the woman who has known the dark and cold,
this is you, the woman who lived the story told.
you found your way, you clung to life,
now just live and love and be,
this is your time to fly;
strong woman just believe.

Welcome

here in the quiet of the morning I think I hear my voice,
untethered, unencumbered, inaudible in noise
but it's there like a drum—like a trickle; beating and steady,
coming from a place within asking if I'm ready.
and in the quiet of this morning I can feel it in my bones,
that the woman I'm becoming will always be my home.
to answer her, myself, I am ready; to listen and to speak,
to stand strong in these bones—to be enough for me.
I see my raw and beautiful and all it took to find this peace
I am grateful, I am humbled, I know it did not come with ease.
and so, I met me on a quiet morning
between the silence and the noise,
and vowed to breathe with only love deep into this voice.

Strange

it's strange.
the empty, damp, and dark feeling dwelling in the middle,
there's so much to be thankful for yet I think of it so little.
and the dark, damp, and empty take over droplets at a time,
until I'm someone in the mirror that I don't recognize.
I stare watching shallow eyes
that hold the depths of many graves,
I say nothing to her questions as she lures me to her cave.
and here I'm standing in the middle of the damp, dark,
and empty,
where the air is damp
the cave is dark
and I am empty.

Virus

if a virus were a ghost he'd be haunting in the halls
he'd be creeping under doors and reaching through the stalls.
if a virus were a villain he'd be a masked hello
he'd leave you feeling feverish and stay with you when you go.
if a virus were visible we'd see him splashing all around,
lapping at our shoe strings, diving into crowds,
but we sit here holding masks and think the virus doesn't know,
all the while he's been watching and he is everywhere we go.

Going In Blind

it's cold
and I'm cold
and I'm tired,
but sleep doesn't come when you're wired.

waiting for the next thing because when it hits
it will hit hard,
and I know it will come crashing
and it will find us where we are.

because from this there is no hiding—this is real life
this is real
we try to keep pretending, try to mask the fear we feel.

it's collective, it's communal
though there may be separate roots,
this uneasiness is present—it's in everything we do.

despite the distance and the news,
despite the facts and all the "truths"
we are in it in this moment,
whatever "it" is it is open

and it's messy and we're covered
in this sticky space in time,
and we don't know where we're headed
because we're going in this blind.

A Little at a Time

it's getting to me I think
a little at a time,
some days it's my body, some days it's my mind

it can feel it like waves of sadness
like tears that just keep falling,
but there are no tears and there's all this madness,
and this feeling just keeps calling

it didn't seem like this at first, I mean it did
but somehow didn't
I had faith and maybe still do, only now it feels hidden
and each day comes with a little more rain
and each night falls with a little more pain

we're all here spinning in the very same wheel
but we're miles apart in the hurt that we feel
it's something for all of us—a thing we can share
it's what makes us human, the fact that we care.

it's getting to me, I think, a little at a time,
some days it's my body,
some days it's my mind.

Envy and Awe

the trees move softly in the wind
reminding me to bend
be less rigid; go with the flow
but I stand staring at them
with a mixture of envy and awe
that one could only hold for trees.
I too feel the wind
but I pin my hair so it will not blow
I straighten my back so I can stand strong
I brace myself so that I am prepared
but I am the fallen one
staring back up at the trees as they bend with the breeze
knowing they have a space carved for themselves
a place where they belong
as I do not.
and so I lay beneath them
pins fallen
limbs loose
and I hold that mixture of envy and awe
close to the bones that rest on the roots

When She Goes

flames climb and roar with a ferocity
unmatched
waves pour over lands claiming what was hers
before returning to the sea
and mountains collapse
as we live and lay and love on this land
that is not ours, but is our home
and we collect our ruins in bottles on shelves
and reflect on the moments that made these memories our own
centuries have collected leaving dust on our bones
but, where then I wonder, will we be when she goes?

False Hope

with false hope and deliverance
from the demons in my past
I chase you blindly and with a passion
that only the hopeless have
in fragments you find me
as I fail to fill in the cracks
knowing once you notice
there will be no coming back.

Call Me Chaos

I am moments unaccounted for
sweet silences forgotten
I am walks through a well lit parking lot
with fresh produce in a sustainable bag
coffee and morning rain
I am Sunday slow and they call me calm
but I am chaos
before the call comes
the fruit drops
the storm breaks
before Monday
and it all starts
again

Wouldn't It Be Lovely

"wouldn't it be lovely"
she let her words float into the space
where wishes meet with prayers
where fears are only colors but truly hold no place
"I am finally ready"
she sent her words off with a force
meant to find the makers, the changers,
the ones in charge of her
"I am free of wanting"
she stated and she claimed
but the words only forsook her
as they sank their talons in her name
"I am waiting, I am patient"
she tore these words out of her bones
forcing herself to trust in the mother,
that the mother would know her own

Constant Reminders

the rest of my days will be filled
with constant reminders of you
there will be small containers filled with shades of eyeshadow
you won't be able to see
trinkets from places only you would know how to find
that are equal amounts beautiful and meaningful
enough to keep in the places of a home
frequented.
there will be napkins from a town in France
that find their place at my table
at the seat where you've sat so many times before
that will sometimes get stained—but I won't be able to call you
some things I will have to channel you for
and figure out on my own now
the rest of my days will be filled
with constant reminders of you
and some days the tears will fall and my heart will clench
while others
I'll smile and laugh and think of something funny
or practical you would say
and it will cheer me up.
until the next time,
when a small case of eyeshadow tucked
in the back of a vanity drawer
makes an unexpected appearance
and somehow feels exactly like losing my breath.

Dragons of a Heart

I follow you like seasons, like secrets in the dark
I follow you in pieces and give you every part
you will always be what haunts me
what has marked my skin in red
you will never truly know me
ever present in my head
funny how the truth can be so ugly and so dark
and sometimes eyes cannot see past the dragons of a heart.

After All This Time

after all this time I found me
but I had no idea who I'd be
turns out I'm laughing in the forest
hiding beneath the trees

I became this woman
unfamiliar
how are her and I the same?
connected only in a mirror
together only in our change

I know I found me
but the wonder
is left burning in my heart
I am who I wanted then, but now
I think I may have fallen apart.

It's Hard to Believe

it's hard to believe
we were there once.
occupying this one space
until life came with its waves
and washed us away
into different corners
and faraway moments.

before we knew it we were back
in this one space
with the shared face
of grief or love or greed

in cycles we find ourselves
in faraway moments
knowing nothing of who we were
but a tiny shared memory
and a force
that pulls us toward the ones who once shared our spaces.

Beside the Glass

when a face you've known for ages
becomes more clear in a single moment
than it has ever been in any collection of moments
and wings break through jagged bone
to show you—what you've known
isn't always all that's true
isn't any more than what's been perceived or imagined by you

when letting go feels like dropping stones
that weight more than all the weight
you've ever carried or known
and you become a little less theirs and a little more your own

when it happens and all the surrounding sounds
become more distinguished
than they have ever been in any collection of moments
every clanking glass, every unfamiliar laugh
punctuating this moment—of clarity

and you know in your core that all you've known before
lives only in the places of the past
and you leave this place, this moment,
like you're leaving your old skin folded in the napkin
beside the glass

You Cannot Write My Story

you cannot write my story
because I wrote it all for you
you cannot tell my secrets
because they are your truths
you cannot live without me
because I am your bones
and they will never know us truly;
in the ways we should be known

Like Gin

I know it in my bones
the way a candle knows a flame
I know it in my soul
it's in the way you say my name

like liquid it rolls off your tongue
smooth like honey
pure like gin
and in the silence where your voice last fell
I could feel you creeping in

and like a game where you have the only advantage
I play along blind and willingly damaged
with nails you lock down my heart
you secure it as your own spare part

and leave me only with the silence
and the space between the noise
that lingers with the ever present
echoes of your voice

Though You May Not Remember

I will know you in the way you show me
the sides of you that are true
I will find you in the smallest moments
when the joy is yours and you're simply you
I will seek you in the crowds we occupy
because there's a piece of you, you leave
like a secret only I can find and you reveal yourself to me
though you may not remember,
I have a heart that beats for you
and I keep it safe in this world of wonder
because you are all that will ever be true.

Home Town

it's the kind of town where banks go to become
long forgotten abandoned buildings

where the store on the corner
is a revolving door of candy that smells like fish or
discount mattresses stacked and packed and waiting

where even the graffiti is somehow less vibrant or meaningful
than it is anywhere else
the kind of town where drugs are sold
in the same place ten year olds buy cigarettes
for their passed out moms
and the moms who aren't passed out
buy sugary promises for their children

it's a town where no one would wish to grow up
but aren't entirely sorry that they did
because there's learning on the sidewalks
and behind the buildings
that can't be taught in schools

it's a town that breeds poets and artists
and children with dreams
housed with sadness and madness and too little heat

but it's a town nonetheless where I carved my name
in the sidewalk that day (that has since been repaved)
and it's a town where I grew and learned that roots aren't for shaming
and it's the town that I know has undeniably shaped me

If Nothing Else

live like wings
will never fail you
like all the places
you wish to see
are explorations you will get to
are places you will be
and when those roots
come pressing for you
and those trees look
strong and true
find your wings
before you're planted
if there's nothing else you do

Only the Taken

I imagine the sunlight
crashing over you
in waves of darkness
as you claw beneath it all
screaming those screams
of silence
and irreverence
that only the taken can hear
I imagine the clouds that cry
opening the sky
to find
a light that doesn't burn you
and in this feeble attempt
you dig deeper
retreating behind
all that is empty and forgotten
like the abandoned dreams
and silent screams
that only the taken can hear

Pills and Promises

pills and promises
you didn't know that you were making
became mine, and theirs,
and yours for the taking
all none the wiser
to the looks and the warnings
as they bounced off of our drab attire
as if resistant to our mourning
decades found us worlds apart
and in the dirt under my fingernails I see you
not as you were, then
but as you are

Like a Beast

I lay sullen
and unopened
like a beast that's yet to grow
my face fallen
words unspoken
a lioness lost
a seed unsown

Never In My Life

never in my life had, I
had a lesser dose of love
inside
from the wanting
to the waiting
to the being filled with hating
never in my life had, I
wanted more than love
for me
inside
but when all expected love
is kept
locked in a chest that fear protects
there is only
hoping
and yearning and eventually learning
that never in my life had, I
known I had all I'd ever need inside.

Origin Story

I am the fair skinned daughter
of an olive skinned man
the first born to a girl
not ready, unplanned

I am the woman
stemmed from a child scorned
held hostage in the home
to which I was born

steeped in violence
and anger
cradled with guilt
and shame
a child who children
saw wasn't the same

countless schools
and towns
doctors
and drugs
a mother who couldn't be woken for hugs

the moves and the many
who witnessed the ways
saw what they saw and
let it be, let her stay

saved by the grace of
my father's mother
who loved me with a love
that led me to discover

that I wouldn't trade the worry
the hunger or the pain
if it meant a single part of now
wouldn't be the same

Shatter Me

shatter me scatter me
clear to the moon
turn my bones into a garden
and my heart into a room
find your home within my soul
let my spirit be your guide
don't let me be forgotten
just because I've died

After All

in the darkest of corners
covered in dust
rests another version of the two of us;
timeless, unburdened, hopelessly small,
I know a place, darling, where we made it after all.

To Remember You By

you left me with something to remember you by
the feathers, the letters, the tears in my eyes
you set your sails toward a different sea
and I'm as loved as I'll ever be.

Vulnerable

your words like waves
sent shocks of awareness
crashing down on me

like warm welcome hurricanes
in an otherwise frozen environment

your willingness to be raw
and wide open
spilled out before you
and I could feel the walls falling
as your voice enveloped us

A Letter to My Life

a letter to my life thus far,
in all these thirty years
you've wrapped me in anxieties and dosed me well with fears
you've also given sunsets, and rises worth the waking
you've shown me love in many forms
and have reminded me that taking
is just the same a part of life as anything we're given
you've kept up the adventure in this guessing game of living
you've seasoned joy with heartache
and have muddied many flowers
you've shown me what it is to know that I do hold the power
in all the control you've handed me,
you've pulled back with such force
as if to prove its all for show, and the power is truly yours
and though you keep it moving,
there are times it feels quite stagnant
like the stillest waters couldn't compare
with the lack of what is happening
perhaps it's by design of course,
i don't doubt you have your reasons,
but I'd like to thank you humbly, for the gift of thirty seasons.

Elementary

the smell of plastic
and pages
lined the air
notes of sloppy Joes
and sweat
lingered in the corners
a hint of crushed crayon
and new sneakers
would greet you
and all of these scents would meet you
ever present behind the doors of brick and steel
and time

She Has Bloomed

she is red wine and dinner parties
dark wood and soft lighting
the faint scent of lemon

she is cedar in the closets
a vegetable garden and take out
all natural cleaner (and a little bit of bleach)

she is patchouli and eucalyptus
vanilla and cardamom
coffee beans and incense
clad in turquoise and drapery

she is Nut milk with a side of eggs
"Gypsy" playing in the background
white curtains blowing in the breeze

she was planted in a mix of pain and mud and coffee
she has bloomed

Who Am I in Your Story?

I'll never know who I am to you now
or who I was to you then
but you'll always be a memory to me
a little lover
a little friend

Life

it carries on in cities and pages
in new names and phases
in gas station bathrooms behind a stall
you've never seen
in holidays and all The Wednesdays in between
in the cracks on the sidewalk where the sand
has been collecting
in the box in the attic full of all you've been forgetting
in the wake of the heavy there will always be light
because it carries on; this still—ness of life.

This River Runs

this river runs
old and cold and new
through years and stones
and moves and homes
and on it pushes through

this river holds
the winter's bones
beside the moss and foam
and spring pours in the way it has
for all the lives it's known

this river watches,
cascading answers
into pools
and hope and hands
and all it knows
is everything—
yet still she has her plans.

Close the Window

when all of our nothingness combined
has left us depleted and curious of a world beyond our own
when the window has been opening a little more each night
and our walls have felt less and less like home
we find ourselves at a precipice
a moment where the window could open a little more—
just enough to hang the sheets we've tied
just enough to breathe and climb
and down one of us will go
while the other stands watching
not alarmed because they'd know
because they wondered too
and longed too to go
and here at the window I wonder would it be me
or would it be you?
so I close the window and resolve to wonder another year
to try journaling or rekindling or whatever else I come by
from now until then
when presumably the window opens again

Chipping Blue

my nails were painted a chipping blue
when the miles found us on separate roads
and there was nothing I could do

over the years the roads cleared and miles closed their gap
my nails were painted a glossy red the day that you came back

and here we are again on our ever winding road
collecting all the miles that will separate our souls

my nails were white on the day I discovered
what really kept us apart
it was never the fault of the roads or the miles
it's always been your heart

Who Saves You

you are more than what they've made you darling,
you are more than bones and lace
there are depths to you—like oceans
your soul can never be replaced
your strength is in the mirror, darling
always bravely staring back
prepared for what they hand you, darling
you will rise as they attack

you are infinite in every sense
you are sunsets on the sea
you are ocean storms and rivers run
through towns that will always be

you are lifeblood and magic
intricate and unique
you cannot be dulled, darling
by a world that doesn't see.

force your light and force your fire
into the tiny space they gave you
hold your head high, keep your fight strong
you will always be who saves you.

Sarah Joannidi is a poet, teacher, and native New Englander. She has been using poetry as her greatest escape since the age of eight. Having had a childhood on the dark side of lovely, *Seedling* is her first published collection, carefully curated using pieces that explore life after childhood trauma, the unexpectedly challenging road to motherhood, and all the beautiful simplicity in between.

www.ingramcontent.com/pod-product-compliance
Lightning Source LLC
Chambersburg PA
CBHW051700040426
42446CB00009B/1237